To:
Ron

Aug. 1975

Much love

(Aunt) Bettielue

INDIANA'S BIG TOP

INDIANA'S
BIG TOP

Don L. Chaffee

FOREMOST PRESS, INC.

Grand Rapids, Michigan

CONTENTS

INDIANA'S BIG TOP

THE GREAT WILNO

VALLEYFIELD P.Q. Aug 1939. Photo E.I. Reg.
—E. GENDRON—

Chapter 1

THE GREAT WILNO

July 20, 1968 was a hot day in Peru, Indiana. Jon Witten lowered his camera from eye level. He was not too sure that he had 'snapped' at the right second to catch the dummy flying out of the cannon's mouth. He had arrived early to take his position in front of the Peru Motor Lodge, an excellent vantage point for taking pictures of the saturday morning parade.

Jon, born some fifty plus years ago in this little Indiana town, considered it a privilege and a pleasure to return here at least once a year for the 'Circus City Days.'

The town, like Jon, had grown a little pudgy. For instance; the city fathers had seen fit to place huge curbside flower boxes at strategic points along the Broadway business section. These boxes filled with earth trying to grow various flowers and small trees served to divert the passing wayfarer's attention from his concrete path. The path too, in many locations, was slightly deteriorated by the elements, the passage of time and many feet.

This being a very warm morning Jon decided to wander over to a local 'watering place' for a bit of refreshment. Another thing this town had was a varied selection of many 'understanding' bars.

Jon's penguin waddle carried his bowling pin carcass to the nearest oasis. His prominent rotund belly was a physical feature that provided him with an amazing capacity for beer and all other forms of liquid including hard booze. His daily consumption of alcohol will preserve him for the ages. He's hardly ever ill. About the only time he gets sick is when the Pizza, Pickles, Chili and liquor hold a council of war in his gut to determine which way to go.

Jon ambled into the 'Circle' and over to the bar. He hooked his thumbs under his belt, shrugged his shoulders and shook his hips to settle his fat ass deeper into his pants — then raising his hands over his head in the gesture of 'I'M The Greatest.' He said: "Gimmie A Drink!"

He set gingerly down on the bar stool and while gently

twirling his glass wondered if he might have missed the picture of the flying dummy. Maybe so. But he would never forget that day, when as a small boy, he stood pop-eyed and opened mouth gazing with rapt wonder at the human body sailing gracefully through the air.

The Great Wilno, the human cannon ball, had just emerged from the huge barrell with a loud 'Boom' and a cloud of smoke. Approaching a speed of eighty miles an hour he turned a beautiful summersault in the air and landed on his back in a net a hundred and some odd feet in front of the cannon's mouth.

One wonders about the origin of this act and even now The Great Wilno gives it considerable thought during his leisure moments. He sometimes asks himself if he would do it over again if he had the chance and even though the answer is usually yes he ponders the thought. Knowing what he knows now things would be considerably different. It still rankles him how he was cheated for many weeks by his agent who pocketed fifteen hundred of Wilno's two thousand dollar a week salary and all because he didn't understand English.

Wilno was and still is a very small and light build for a man. His mother used to say that she could raise bigger muscle lumps in her cheese sauce than he could in his arms. His father knew he could never stand a hardy life so he encouraged his son to be a watch maker. His Dad even offered to send him to college and provide the tools of the trade.

He tried it for three years and found it very boring. He finally told his Dad that he didn't like the watch making trade and wanted something more exciting like joining a circus. This irked the old man no end who said:

"If you leave this house to join the circus don't ever come back and tell me 'you don't like that either.' "

He didn't go back for five straight years.

In 1922 he started out with a small circus that was then touring Germany. They agreed to teach him the art of acrobatics such as tumbling and the trapeze. He signed a contract for a two year period of time that only guaranteed him his living. After the expiration of the contract they were to put him on a small salary in addition to his board and keep. This was Wilno's introduction to 'show business.'

Many nights in Germany he went to bed cold and hungry. On week-ends when show people had a chance to relax and freshen up a bit in a hotel he couldn't enjoy this luxury. No money. But being a persistent youth of only twenty years he stuck it out and continued to learn all he could about his chosen profession.

It didn't take him long to realize that with three or four people in the act there just wasn't enough money to go around, you had to divide the salary too many ways. He decided he wanted it all so he quit that show, perfected his own act and took it to England. It was while he was playing at the Hippodrome in London that he met the lady with the cannon act. This act fascinated him and the year 1926 was the turning point of his life.

At the time the woman explained the act to him she was in her seventies and retired. She showed him many pictures of the act and told him how it was done by using a small cannon that shot her into the air about twenty feet to a trapeze. He studied this idea for some time and realized that if it could be enlarged upon it should have a terrific impact on the public. He just couldn't get the idea out of his mind so after finishing his London contract he refused other engagements. He had decided to become a 'human cannonball.'

He went back to Berlin and hired an engineer. Together they pored over many ideas and designs of their own. Wilno knew he was taking tremendous risks with life, his own, and he wanted to make damn sure that everything would work out right. They had to create enough power to hurtle a human body through the air X number of feet and land uninjured in a net. That was the eingineer's problem and he finally convinced his boss that he had it all figured out and his formula was infallible. They built the cannon.

The first shot took place in Germany in 1927 and was a great success, from there on in he figured he had it made. He worked in Germany through 1928 and in 1929 he opened in Paris France. In March a booking agent from New York saw his act in Paris, got excited and said to him:

"Wilno — I want you for the United States."

Wilno finished the balance of his engagement in Paris and then cancelled the rest of his contracts to appear in Europe, but of course his booking agent had to buy off a few of the contracts. Together with his agent Wilno arrived on the East coast of the United States in May of 1929.

It was in Syracuse New York that he had his first accident. Through some miscalculation of his power setting he failed to attain enough height and necessary speed to land in the middle of the net. But in falling short he did manage to grasp the edge of the net with his extended fingers and break his fall, otherwise it would have proved very disastrous, as it was he only broke his shoulder instead of his neck.

He had a contract to perform so Wilno persuaded his assistant to take over the job of 'human cannonball.' To lessen the risk a bit for the assistant they pushed the cannon closer to the net and lowered the pressure.

The assistant made two successful shots but on the third one disaster struck again. He was killed in Springfield Mass.

At the command of "Attention-Fire" the understudy must have fainted and therefore was too relaxed. He never fully emerged from the barrel, his body hung part way out of the cannon's mouth. Forty thousand people in the Grand Stand started yelling:

"Let the barrel down!"

Wilno did and his assistant's body fell out of the cannon's mouth to the ground, landing on his back, but this was not the cause of death.

At the command of "Fire!", one's body must be very stiff and tense, you cannot be the least bit relaxed. If you are, the compression and pressure pushes you together just like an accordion and cramps your body. This is what happened to Wilno's assistant. When the pressure hit him it broke every bone in his body.

Some people thought that Wilno, through carelessness, was the cause of this so the police impounded his cannon. The investigation lasted approximately six weeks. The assistant was buried in Springfield and his personal belongings sent back to Germany.

Perhaps at this point we should explain a bit about the hazards of the act. The principal is the same as launching a plane from an aircraft carrier. A catapult in other words.

The noise and smoke of the explosion is merely window-dressing. Inside the barrel of the cannon the man stands on a plate beneath which are compressed heavy springs, and, in later years a cylinder of compressed air was used.

As the trigger is pulled a charge of gunpowder is simultaneously fired creating the sound and smoke. The springs or the compressed air provide the power to send the man on his way. Danger is present as you do go through a certain amount of heat and smoke even though you don't realize it. Your speed is so great that you don't even hear the explosion. Your initial speed approaches eighty miles per hour.

If the shot is out in the open at a carnival or a fair you have to consider the wind direction and velocity in order to properly place the net. When you leave the mouth of the cannon and are in the air you control your body by positioning your arms and legs in such a manner that you will be in the proper attitude at the right moment to land on your back in the net. The landing is the most important part of the whole act. That net is pretty hard if you hit it in the wrong body position.

In making a high shot of sixty feet or so the barrel is elevated at about a fifty degree plus angle. Wilno sometimes had blackouts caused by the lift-off. The pressure was so great that it forced the blood from his head into the lower part of his body — but he had to recover quick enough to control his landing in the net. Serious injury or death is the price of poor body control.

Here was Wilno, a German boy in an English speaking country. But he did have an interpreter with him some of the time. He didn't realize how he could have made enough money in ten years to retire on. His booking agent really took him to the cleaners.

The act was booked for two thousand dollars a week, but Wilno didn't know that, the agent gave him only five hundred dollars a week and pocketed the rest. When he finally learned the language and found out about the injustice perpetrated on him he fired his agent.

The first year or so in this country was pretty disheartening for our Mr. Wilno — the human cannon ball. But having his assistant killed in the act and his agent taking three fourths of his salary still didn't make him give up — he continued on with the tradition that "the show must go on."

The spring of 1930 found him in Peru, Indiana. He signed up with the American Circus Corporation. He then joined the Hagenbeck and Wallace show, one of the circuses owned by the corporation, and stayed with them through the 1932 season. At this time most of the circuses were owned by Ringling's corporation and he was somewhat of a hard man to work for. The corporation was always trying to cut down on the salaries paid the performers and other personnel. A sort of a dog-eat-dog business.

Wilno was pretty ambitious and he felt he was making too little for the amount of publicity he was bringing to the show. His act was the last one on the program and the crowd always stayed to see him perform. Never-the-less the circus corporation kept cutting his salary until he finally refused to sign any more contracts.

The circus corporation retaliated by trying to get him deported from his adopted country. He even had a letter from Washington D.C. giving him the name of the ship, stateroom number and date of his departure from this country. He was very hurt by all of this. Especially because of the fact that all of the money he made here he spent here. He never sent any of his money back home to Germany.

Wilno's friends rallied around him. The congressman from his district and the governor of the state came to his aid. He received a two year extension on his passport. The circus corporation was unsuccessful in getting him deported and he is still living here today.

After leaving the circus in 1932 Wilno mounted his cannon on a truck that he purchased for four thousand dollars. He could now go anywhere, at any time and he was strictly on his own. He hired men to work for him and he toured the country appearing at fairs, carnivals and Shrine shows.

With the passage of time Wilno began to have severe back-aches. The doctor told him it was caused by the compression and tension of the shots. He finally had to give it up so he trained a new assistant to take over. During the course of human events the assistant got pretty big for his britches and wanted ninety percent of the take. Wilno decided to retire from the business. They made their last shot in New Orleans at the Shrine circus in 1948 and then returned to Peru.

The Wilnos love their adopted country and believe there is no better place on earth. Two or three years ago, during a Christmas Holiday, they went back to Germany to see his folks. He still has four sisters living there.

And now they are enjoying their retirement years puttering around their small farm amongst the many people they call friends here in Peru Indiana.

JOE REED

Chapter 2

POLE MAN   *Joe Reed*

Joe Reed stepped out of the air-conditioned comfort of the bank onto the hot sidewalk. "Simba N'Golo Sui." (Too darned hot.) He muttered to himself as he headed down the street to his place of employment.

The job he had now as a swamper in a saloon was a far cry from the glamour of his youthful circus days. His 77 years didn't seem to slow him down very much as he kept pace with the parade that was proceeding in an orderly fashion down Broadway.

Joe was pretty proud of his little town as he called it. He had spent most of his life in and around Peru. He always returned after the Circus season on the road to winter here. Mopping his sweaty brow with the sackfull of change he was carrying he shouldered his way through the crowd to the curb-stone.

The parade had momentarily halted to let a huge German Shepard take a crap in the middle of the street. His handler, standing beside the dog, tried to look nonchalant as he listened to the jeers of the spectators. Joe grinned, turned and resumed his own march down the street towards the air-conditioned comfort of Mavrick's.

Joe never gave much thought to his sartorial status. He wore clothes as a matter of necessity and usually disregarded color combinations if the garmets were comfortable. There was enough room in his pants for his ample belly and enough slack in the seat that you could drop a cat through them without scratching his butt.

The gray broad-banded suspenders draped over a gaudy orange and yellow checkered shirt held the kaki pants at half mast. He had the appearance that if somebody hollered "Boo" and scairt him he could cut and run un-impeded and leave a pile of clothes behind him.

Joe, the oldest of eleven children, never married. He was born in Washington D.C. and he spent twenty two years traveling the length and breadth of the United States. He loved the circus. Now, in his retirement, drawing social

17

security and making a few nickels working for Mavrick he enjoys life. God never put breath into a more tolerant or understanding man. And Joe often reminisces.

"They called us 'Razorbacks' in those days, alls we did was load and unload the show to and from the trains. The 'Roustabouts' handled the canvas; set up and tore down the tents and man-handled the bleachers.

My job was pole-man. It took a lot of skill to guide those heavily loaded wagons up and down the steel 'runs' or ramps as the circus was loading or unloading the trains. To guide the vehicle I would encircle the wagon tongue with my left arm and hand, then grab the 'gooseneck' or ring with my right hand and thus steer the wagon up or down the ramp.

There were 'Pull-up' teams of horses to supply the power. I'll never forget the time I got hurt on this job back in 1926 in Des Moines, Iowa. Broke my leg. I was on the Sells Floto show at the time and was laid up in the hospital for over a month. Finally caught up with the show in Denver, Colorado. This was the only time I was hurt in 22 years with the circus.

"The Hagenbeck and Wallace show was the first circus I joined. Then the Ringling show for a year, then John Robinson's show; from there to Sells Floto — stayed with them until they went on the shelf in 1932. Then back to Hagenbeck for the years of 1933-4-5. Yes sir twenty two years in the circus business and I loved every minute of it.

"One thing about the circus, it was one big happy family. Everyone was equal — white, black red or brown; Razorback, roustabout, animal handlers, trainers and star performers. Everybody had a job to do and when their job was finished another crew took over to continue 'On with the show'.

"The food was always of the best, excellent in other words and you could eat all you wanted. Everybody ate the same food, all prepared in the same cook tent. I've seen some of them colored boys eat a dozen eggs and a pound of bacon for breakfast, you could send your plate back as many times as you wanted to."

"Never worried too much about sleep, you slept wherever and whenever you could, if you kept yourself pretty clean you had bunks to sleep in — even the workers, course you had to take turns while the other guy was working. The performers had their coaches and the really tough 'Rowdys' slept under the wagons.

"Always looked forwards to starting out on the road in the spring, usually around the middle of March. We would stay out through the fall and sometimes even through Christmas.

The Coliseum in Chicago was the first stop and then we'd work our way west and back through the country to the east in the fall and then later through the south. I'll never forget the year 1925 on Christmas day in Houston, Texas as that marked the longest season we had ever played. The day after Christmas we started back to our winter quarters here in Peru, Indiana. And, on our arrival it was sure cold, blustery and snowing.

"At that time there were three shows wintering here in Peru. 'Hagenbeck and Wallace', 'John Robinson' and 'Sells Floto.' The Ringling show wintered in Baraboo Wisconsin until their winter quarters burned down and they moved the winter quarters to Sarasota, Florida.

"Time never hung very heavy on my hands even during the long stands when we stayed in one town for a few days — and then of course in the winter quarters when we was holed up for quite a spell I always had lots of booze and women. Didn't miss many women, if I did they wasn't worth havin. Of course some people was always broke and couldn't have any fun cause they couldn't save up any money for a blast. But these folks knew the circus would take care of them — give them a place to sleep and plenty to eat winter and summer.

"I usually managed to save a little — I could usually land in winter quarters with seventeen or eighteen hundred dollars. Course I used to gamble some, Poker, dice — though I didn't fool with poker much. I'se a dice man, bones that is — we always called them bones and I used to be pretty lucky with them, that is after I learned how. When I first started playing way back when I'se a kid I thought you went to a crap game with a roll of toilet paper.

"Oh we had our troubles. Fights, once in a while you'd hear the cry 'Hey Rube.' Then all the circus people would grab a tent stake, bottle or whatever was handy and head for the melee. The town rough necks usually started it by cutting our tent ropes or tormenting the performers but the circus boys always won the fight. Once in a while a storm would get pretty violent and the tents would blow down. It would be chaos for a while but we'd all pitch in and with the elephants helping we soon had them set up once more.

"That time in Canada back in 1926 was a duezy — during a big storm all the elephants stampeded and it took us a solid week to round them all up. The damn things got out into the woods and we even had the Indians on the show out ridding their horses around the countryside looking for them. Finally herded them all togehter again except one mean old bull that we had to shoot.

"It was back in 1918 that the Hagenbeck and Wallace show had a train wreck up in norther Indiana. An empty troop train ran into the show train. Some of the cars caught fire and there was an awful lot of people hurt and a good many were killed. I remember the ambulances and the undertakers all around picking up the people and putting them in the baskets. Ed Ballard owned the show at that time and he paid the burial expenses for every one of them.

A wide grin spread across Joe's face as he thought about the lions that escaped during the evening show in Chicago's coliseum. The lions just walked around the hippodrome track minding their own business.

"The people were screaming and a-hollering and making a terrible noise but the lion's trainer, old John Elliott, just kept following them around talking German to them and they went right back into their cages. No trouble at all. Those lions only understood German.

"About the saddest thing I recall was what happened to my friend Bessie Smith. She was a colored girl and a great singer in a side show, even the actors of today sing some of her songs and copy her style. She got awful sick in Kansas City back in the 'twenties' and the towns-people wouldn't

20

let her in the hospital because she was colored. She finally died after a lot of sufferin. That sure hurt me. I never got over it, how them white folks treated her—another human being.

"Animal traning. There was a profession that was never dull. Oh them animals knew who was boss alright. There had to be a little cruelty in their training as they had to be taught to obey. They taught bears to dance while they was muzzled and they placed them on hot stones.

"It took about a year to get a group of cats ready to go on the road and you put them through their so called paces every day. I remember Clyde Beatty got clawed a couple of times but he wound up to be a great and wonderful animal trainer. When Clyde was young he used to clean out the cages for old John Elliott on the Robinson show.

"Tom Mix, he was a true cowboy. He used to be a deputy marshall back in Tulsa Oklahoma. I used to work for Tom back in 1929, 30 and 31. This was after his movie career. His horse, Tony, was a beautiful and well trained animal. Tom had his own private railroad car that was really plush. His daughter, Ruth, used to travel with him a great deal. When we'd hit a town she'd say:

'Joe! After you get unloaded will you please bring the Rolls Royce around to the private car? I want to go shopping.'

"Tom Mix was a crack shot. Many's the time I've seen him lay on his back and shoot glass balls hanging from strings swirling around the top of the tent. He'd never miss, course that'd been a little hard to do since he was using bird shot in a six-shooter. That shot pattern was 2-3 feet wide when it got to the top of the tent.

"Tom was not what you'd call stuck up. He'd hob-nob with anybody. He'd always play ball with us colored boys. This was not true with some of the others. Ken Maynard for instance wouldn't associate with the working people. Ken worked on the Cole Brothers show out of Rochester in 1935.

"When Tom Mix left the show for good and went back to California he wanted me to go with him and he offered

21

me a very good salary too. But I couldn't see it as I had a girl here in Peru at that time and she didn't want to go and I didn't want to leave her here alone. I knew I'd be alright here in Peru as long as the Ballards were around as I'd worked for Ed Ballard for years.

"If I had my life to live over again I'd go right back to the circus, it's a great life and I enjoyed every minute of it.

"But I enjoy my retirement here in Peru now amongst my friends and the circus atmosphere that prevails here. I've worked for Mavrick now off and on for thirty one years and with what he pays me and my social security I get along. I don't need much and I'll be happy here 'Till' the day I die."

MR. AND MRS. ART JOHN

Chapter 3

CIRCUS ARTIST   *Art Johns*

Art Johns doesn't go in much for present day circus parades. The last one he rode in of any consequence was down in Indianapolis on a wagon he built himself. The wagon contained two male lions weighing about six or seven hundred pounds. A guy drove up with a six pony hitch drawing a small wagon. He came right alongside Art's wagon containing the lions and they lunged. If that wagon hadn't been built right they would have gone right through the bars. Thank God everything held and the lions just roared.

Art was born in Bunker Hill in the year nineteen hundred. At an early age he realized he had a great talent for art work. Formal education bored him and he stayed in the sixth grade so long they thought he was the janitor. He was what you would call 'Self educated', only sought the knowledge that he was interested in and to hell with the rest of it.

But let Art Johns tell his own story. "When I was young I worked under the world's best Circus Painter — Ernie Sylvester. He taught me how to paint a circus wagon. A good sign painter still is not a circus wagon decorator. He'd make it look like a billboard.

"You have to see the decoration in its entity before you ever start to apply the design on a wagon. I have a schroll work theme that I've used all the way through my circus art career. I call it French Recoco Schroll. The last job I used this on was the Cole Brothers Clyde Beatty circus in Deland Florida. This was back in 1965 when I painted all the side show banners for them.

"The first job I had in 'Show Business' was in 1922 when I painted railroad cars out here in the car sheds. There were three large shows here in winter quarters, the 'Hagenbeck and Wallace, Sells Floto and the John Robinson.

"The only show I ever traveled with was the Cole Brothers Clyde Beatty circus that was organized up north of here in Rochester Indiana back in 1935. They had quite a title for that show:

'Cole Brothers World Toured Circus with Clyde Beatty And Alan King.' This was painted on all the flat cars, coaches, cages and all the equipment wagons — some job.

"On the road I painted all the banners. We had a banner salesman, Jack Mills, that went on ahead of the show and sold the advertising. He would send me a telegram the day before we were to appear in a town telling me at what hotel I was to pick up the copies of the advertising to appear on the banners for that particular town.

"When we arrived in town I would go to the hotel, pick up the copies, grab a cab back to the circus lot and go to work. We had 22 elephants each carrying large banners advertising local business of that particular town. Sometimes our banner salesman would go overboard and I'd have to paint banners to be carried by the camels too.

"All of this had to be accomplished by parade time which was elven AM. And in all my time with the circus I never held up that parade five minutes. I was considered the fastest banner writer in the business.

"You could always tell when a storm was brewing by the way the elephants acted. They seemed to know when a 'Blowdown' was on the way and they would start trumpeting. The worst thing about a 'Blowdown' was that the wind would pick up the tent. It would belly up like a balloon, whipping the center and side poles about hitting the people on the inside of the tent. This never killed anybody but it did injure a few. The people themselves were their own worst enemy by their panic and the trampling of each other in their efforts to get out of the tent.

"My greatest circus hero of all time was Emmett Kelly, the clown, when he was in that fire at Hartford, Conn. with the Ringling Brothers show in July of 1944. Emmett was an old friend of mine.

"Nobody can whip a circus, it just can't be done. I'd like to take a group of circus people and get into some of our present day riots, they'd clean out the rioters in a hurry. Back in the old days a circus usually had an elephant trained to swing a two by four horizontally about three feet above the ground and just keep walking into the mob. Greatest pacifier and mob disperser I ever seen. Sure could cut a wide swath through a crowd.

"One time we were in a town, I won't mention the name of the burg and we got wind of a plot to whip us. I dressed up as a townsman in a stripped shirt and was supposed to join them when they appeared. We always called them the townmonkeys. Well everything went according to our plan.

"We stretched a wire across the path leading to the main entrance of the show. The wire was firmly anchored on one side by the stake wagon and on the other with a chain wagon. When the town toughs showed up I joined them and hollered:

'Come On! Let's go and get them circus bums.'

Well we all started running with me in the lead. When we come to the wire they couldn't see it in the dusk of the evening. I just jumped the wire and kept on running and they hit that wire and went down like ten-pins. The circus 'roustabouts' fell on them, battering the hell out of them with their long chains holding keys. Tent stakes and fists also figured in the melee. The battle didn't last five minutes. The town boys left the lot pronto, beaten, sadder and considerably wiser. Ya, Ya just can't whip a circus.

"Never lived higher on the hog than I did with the circus. The food was always excellent, they raised everything they needed on the farms at the winter quarters, vegtables, pork, beef, chickens and eggs and they threw it on the table. In winter quarters the chef, Geo. Davis, always served fried bread for breakfast. That was just a starter. You still had your choice of bacon and eggs; ham or whatever else you wanted plus all three if you so desired — and all you could eat.

"I'll never forget the first day I went to work at the winter quarters and they treated me so good. I couldn't figure out why. They told me they always treated the newcomers with the greatest respect cause they wanted them to feel at home and enjoy their association with the circus. I felt pretty proud that day to lead the line to the cook house for dinner.

"Unbeknowns to me they had a Billy Goat stationed

just outside the paint shop door and the first one out was bound to get it. I swaggered out the door and — BAM — the goat knocked me silly. That was my welcome to the circus cook house. But the food kinda made up for the indignity, it was the best ever placed on a dinner table.

"The circus was renewed every year in winter quarters. The wagons would be brought into the paint shop by the roustabouts. Wagons were jacked up and the running gear removed both fore and aft. The wheels removed from the axles, the boxes placed on sawhorses. They never removed the old paint, just painted right over it.

"The roustabouts would then paint everything of that particular wagon assembly a solid color yellow, red, white or green. A color pertaining to what ever that wagon was supposed to portray. Then the artist would step in for the decorating relative to whatever the wagon contained such as black mained lions, fighting lions, tigers or performing bears. The artist would paint whatever he saw in his mind's eye. In the winter quarters there was always three or four artists at work on this project. Why! I have put as high as eighteen hundred dollars worth of gold leaf on one wagon, and this during the depression. The only thing you had to know about the wagon was the number and what it was to be used for.

"The wagons were constructed of the finest materials, seasoned hickory, oak and hard maple. They were easy to maneuver on show lots as they were designed so that the front wheels would turn under the body of the wagon. The tongues were wide, up to fourteen inches, so they would stand a lot of side thrust and they could be removed from the wagon by the pulling of one pin. This was necessary for the snug loading of the wagons on the railroad cars.

"Those 'Sunburst' wheels were beautiful. This effect was accomplished by the insertion of webs of wood firmly set between the spokes of the wheel. The wide edge of the web near the rim of the wheel was cut in various designs. The webs together with the spokes were painted all colors of the rainbow. As the wheel revolved the effect was an everchanging flash of color hence the word 'Sunburst'. These wheels could cost up to one hundred fifty to two hundred dollars each and this was back in the days when a dollar was worth a hundred cents.

"Some of those band wagons were huge, twenty two feet long and eight feet high and could cost a couple thousand dollars to build. Weighing tons they required from a six horse to a forty horse hitch to move, though the forty horses were usually more for show purposes.

"Spalding and Rogers perhaps had the first forty horse hitch back in 1848. It was driven by a J. W. Paul. In 1866 the Yankee Robinson show had one as did the Dan Rice show in 1873. In 1898 Barnum and Bailey toured Europe with a forty horse hitch of matched greys. In 1903 and 1904 Jake Posey drove a forty horse hitch for James Bailey. While handling this great team Posey had two helpers, one manning the wheel brakes and the other one to keep the lines straight. When he turned a corner twenty feet of leather reins would slide through his fingers. He held ten reins in each hand, one rein for each two horses. It took a lot of precision handling and room to make a turn with such an outfit. One time in Detroit while negotiating a turn the driver noticed a lamp post in the way. After a moments thought he removed the obstacle with a wheel and the wagon rolled merrily along.

"Working for animal trainers and decorating their wagons was always an enlightning experience. I walked into the animal barn one time to paint the cages. The animals were supposed to be quartered elsewhere during the painting process and the cages were spaced all around the barn.

"When I walked in to pick my overhalls off the hook there set a lioness staring me straight in the eye. I never said a word, just backed out, shut the door and went over to tell the trainer he had a lion loose in the cat barn. Didn't bother the trainer much though, he just went over and shooed the lioness into another cage. I wasn't interested in watching the action and I made damn sure after that little episode that the coast was always clear before I sauntered into another cat barn.

"I painted that picture of Tom Mix on the side of the 'Sells Floto show wagon. I can remember when Tom stayed at the local hotel getting drunk and drinking beer out of his hat. You could see lots of different people around that hotel even Unbanga natives from Africa.

"Feeling our oats one day we fixed up a joke on the local police chief. Told him there was a guy down here in the restaurant raising hell so would he please come down and get him and throw him in jail. Our guy was the circus giant seven foot and one inch tall. We had him setting on the floor when the chief came in. We pointed him out to the chief and he went over and placed his hand on the giants shoulder. The giant started to rise and just kept on going up. The chief stared up at him and didn't know whether to shit or go blind.

"Things are not near as exciting around here as they used to be. Cheerful Gardner would periodically bring his elephants downtown for an impromptu parade. It was during one such outing that one of the bulls got disgusted with ambling along his prosaic path so he turned his shuffling tread aside and walked through the cigar store across from the police station. Probabaly felt the need of a chew. The store was a shambles.

"It's just as well that things have quieted down, us old timers couldn't stand the gaff. This retirement is alright and I just paint for pleasure. Oh! I occasionally make scale models of circus equipment on a contract basis. But very little of that now-a-days. I'm just going to enjoy life."

CIRCUS FESTIVAL PARADE 1968

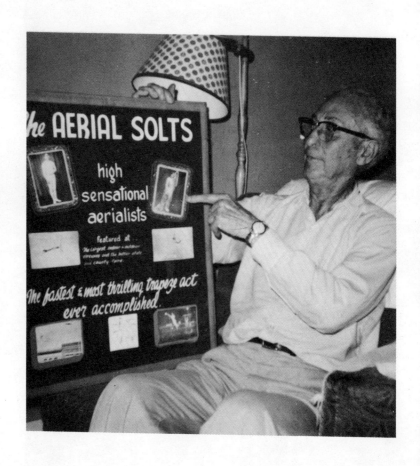

CARL SOLT

Chapter 4

AERIALIST   *Carl Solt*

"Hello Jon! Hot ain't it!" Said Carl Solt as he slapped his friend on the shoulder.

"Sure is, but what are you doing down here Carl? This is a little warm for you isn't it?"

"Nah! You shoulda worked under the big top in the old days. I had-a see this parade. This is one of the very few towns in the country that tries to uphold the tradition of the old time circus and the circus parades. 'Course' it doesn't have any cats or elephants in it, it's too slow and drawn out and the sections are too far apart. But I still think they're making a lot of progress.

"You know I spent all my working life in the circus. Started in back in 1906 doing a tumbling 'free act' for a tent show. I was eight years old at the time and lived in Kansas, went to school in the winter time and performed in the summer. Finally graduated to doing an act on the horizontal bars and from there to a double trapeze act with my brother. We really perfected this act in 1910.

"We joined up with a 'Mud Show' in 1910, this was 'Happy Bills' show, A 'Mud Show' is a circus where all the cages, wagons and equipment is pulled by horses from town to town. There were no 'motorized' trucks in those days and we was too poor to ride the trains.

"At that time there were three such shows on the road. 'Happy Bill, Honest Bill and Lucky Bill.' Lucky Bill was the father of Happy Bill and Honest Bill and they all operated out of Kansas. All three of them were a one ring circus.

"By this time my brother and I were quite good on the horizontal bars and we were paid twelve dollars a week apiece plus our food and a place to sleep.

"Just about the time things were cruising along in good shape my brother decided to quit so we left 'Happy Bills' show and went back to live in our sister's hotel with our mother. That meant going back to school.

"The circus life was instilled too deep in my blood stream and I was itching to get back to the show. 'Happy

33

Bill' offered me the opportunity and an additional entice-ment of working 'Chief', a mean old bull elephant. Mother didn't want me to go but finally conceded to my wishes when I told her. 'If you let me go now, then you will know where I am at. If you don't let me go then I'll run away and you'll never know where I am. Well she finally gave me her permission to rejoin the circus.

" 'Happy Bill' was as good to me as he promised and I rode that mean old elephant, 'Chief', all over the country from town to town. In addition to that I worked him on the show pushing wagons, pulling tent stakes when the show was over and packing up for the trip to the next town.

"He was a mean old cuss and you had to watch him as he would roll up his trunk and belt you one. When we would come to a bridge 'Chief' would place a foot on it and gradually increase the pressure, if he didn't like the feel he would refuse to cross the bridge. I would then get down off the elephant, Cross the bridge and holler to him to come on over. He would squeal awhile, lumber down the bank beside the bridge and make his way across the river to me.

"He was already trained when I got him and when I left the show old 'Chief' pulled my box of gear over to the depot for me and then I walked him back to the lot and staked him. That elephant respected me and any time I spoke to him he would flap his ears with pleasure. Another trick of old 'Chief's' was when you would pat him under the chin he would beller. Course I would wait until the menagerie tent was full of people and then pat him under the chin. The crowd would sure scamper.

"Somebody convinced me that I needed an education so I left the show again to go back to school for a stretch. That got monotonous so my brother and I worked out a double horizontal bar act and we wound up joining a two car show in Saint Louis.

"We was playing Coffeyville Kansas. This was on a small stage and my brother was doing a somersault be-tween the bars when his feet hit the flys, strips hanging down from the ceiling of the stage. This killed his timing and he fell and broke his leg. The doctor set his leg and we went back home. My brother quit 'show business' for good and I did another stint in school.

"School was very boring, I got very restless and started looking around, finally run across an advertisement of a 'wagon show' looking for a bar act. They were located in Denver Indiana. I wrote to them and they said, 'Come on along.' Of course in the meantime I had tried to keep up my old skills on the trapeze and had perfected a flying ring act.

"The owner of this show had two daughters, the oldest was named Mary. One day he asked me to take her into the act and teach her to be a trapeze performer. She was very able and learned easy. Within three or four weeks our double trapeze act was in the show. I was beginning to enjoy the proximity of feminine companionship and being at the impressible age I asked her to marry me. She accepted. In January of 1916 we were married.

"We stuck with the show for two years and during this time it was having tough sledding. As we were the in-laws everybody got paid but us. We finally decided to leave as we had to make some money so we got in touch with another 'Truck' show. We did double trapeze, and in addition, the wife worked the dogs. I laid out the lots and finally wound up being a sort of an advance man for the show.

"While in Memphis Tennessee I got pretty good on the horizontal bars doing fast doubles and I decided to try a third. Turn, one kick, then another, got half over and fell. Broke my neck, they said I was out for nine hours. I was paralyzed for three weeks and my wife took care of me. We lived in light housekeeping rooms. We finally hooked a trapeze from the ceiling of the back porch so I could stretch my muscles and get back in shape again to join another show.

"When I was ready we contacted the M. L. Clark show and they took us on, even paid us two weeks in advance to help us get back on our feet financially. Our landlady wouldn't take the back rent, said we could send it along after we had worked for a while.

35

While we were on the Clark show a Mr. Bert Bowers of the Hagenbeck and Wallace shows offered us the opportunity of joining their show. They wanted us to perform on the double bars, trapeze and the perch act. We had recently perfected the perch act in 1920.

"The perch act consisted of a thirty foot pole that I balanced with the aid of a belt around my waist. The pole is in a perpendicular position with my wife performing on the top of the pole. We rehearsed this act for about three days and was ready for the show. We opened in Louisville and Mr. Bowers raised our salary an extra ten dollars a week for this extra act we threw in. We were only supposed to do this act until he could get another act to replace it. He said it would be a short time, but we wound up doing the perch act all season.

"That was the year that I believe I was the only person doing three acts in the center ring. We started out doing the perch act in the No. one ring with the double trapeze and the aerial bar act in the center ring. The next town we showed in — Findlay Ohio, they put the perch act in the center ring. This put all our three acts in the coveted center ring. Naturally this caused a bit of jealousy among the other performers.

"Yes! We'd experience a few bad storms on rare occasions. The violent ones we called 'Blowdowns.' One time we were performing at the top of the tent when the bars started to jump and twist. Stokes, a comedy man, hollers 'I'm getting out of here.' and he jumped into the net. We all thought it a good idea so we jumped after him — a sort-of-a-leap-for-life. Our boss canvassman, Jack Curtis, put out extra rigging, guy ropes and held the tent.

"The cry 'Hey Rube', this was in Mississippi. A small town show had preceded us into this burg by about three weeks. Students from a nearby college had cut her down, cut the tent ropes that is. We knew about this and was prepared for them. We tied white handkerchiefs around our arms so we'd know the circus people and not clobber each other in the melee. At the cry 'Hey Rube' we all grabbed stakes, elephant hooks, chains and whatever was handy. We really worked those townfolk over in a manner they

36

wouldn't forget right away. Believe me, they had to carry them away in cars. But all in all we had very few fights considering the time I spent with the circus.

"The Ballard family including Chad and his sister would visit the show occasionally and whenever this happened the word would go out to the performers to wear your best custom and do your very best. 'The Ballards are in the press box.' So believe me we wore our best and we done our damdest.

"Henry, the Japanese cook, traveled with the Ballards in their private car — 'Lost River'. That was always the last car on the train. Eventually Henry decided to go back home to Japan to die and it took him quite awhile to round up his money that he had stashed away in banks throughout the country. But he did go home with a lot of Jingling pockets.

"The first thing you learn in a trapeze act is how to hit the net. If in returning to the bar and you miss, you try to hit the net on your stomach with outstretched arms. If you are in a somersault and you miss the catcher you try to land on your back.

"That's how Ernie Lane was killed. He was doing a triple somersault and lost control of himself, missed and hit the net on the back of his neck — broke it and died a day later.

"We had good sleeping accommodations on the trains. Married couples had the lower berths and the singles were in the uppers. The morality was very good, never no trouble.

"Wife had a dog act in our 'Sundown' years. Others had trained the dogs but she watched them, learned the routine and took over. The dogs liked her and she got along very well with them. I once trained a dog act and then trained a girl to handle them. And believe me, it was harder to teach the girl than it was the dogs.

"I watched Clyde Beatty a number of times and can remember when he came on the show at the age of sixteen working under a well known animal trainer. There was a little cruelty in training the animals. But they did have to be conquered and the methods were sometimes not so gentle. Once the animal learned what was expected of him you never had much trouble with him from that day on. He would faithfully follow your cue or voice command.

"I'll never forget the time the German Government sent five representatives to live and travel with our circus. They wanted to find out how the circus could feed and handle so many people, animals; Load, unload, tear down and set up in so short a time. And on top of all that, you had a parade at eleven o'clock every morning — the parade was always on time. This was a very efficient operation.

"When Jack Dempsey was still heavy weight champion he came on the show to visit. He was, and still is, a personal friend of mine.

"The last show that I was on the road with was the Hagenbeck and Wallace circus. I retired from there in 1923. From that time on I played fairs and the shrine circus for twenty years. I worked for Warren Davenport, my agent, until 1945 and then retired from all circus activity.

"Well, see ya Jon! Take it easy."

HAROLD A. YOUNG SR.

Chapter 5

THE BANDS *Harold A. Young, Sr.*

"You know Jon, it's surprising how good the youngsters are in these High-school bands," said Harold.

"Here they are on a hot day wearing uniforms with high-choke collars, stepping smartly down the street and, considering their marching, playing pretty damn good music."

"It's a far cry from the circus bands I played in. Most of the time we rode in wagons. Oh they did try bands mounted on horses and various animals but this never worked out too good. Ya got trouble enough playing an instrument without trying to set a horse.

"I started out with the John Robinson show back in 1916 playing a cornet for Dick Masters who was the director of the band at that time. Didn't last too long though as I wasn't good enough. There was an old German playing first chair and I'll never forget the time he told me off down here in Marion.

"This happened on a sunday morning as the two of us was down at the creek washing out our sox. I asked him how I was doing in the band and he said:

'Vel I tell you. You go home and practice three hours a day for three years, then come back and I'll listen to you again.'

"I was sorry I asked."

"After that band episode I went to work for John Moore in the reserved seats and sold concert tickets. My brother and his wife was also with the show doing a trapeze and perch act. I sorta regained my self-esteem. I was a much better ticket seller than I was a cornet player.

"Along about this time Mr. Mugum gave me an excellent opportunity to make some big money and I didn't have sense enough to take advantage of it. He offered me the 'White Ticket wagon'. This was considered a golden opportunity for all circus people as the 'shakedown' was worth a hundred dollars a day.

Jon Whitten turned to look with amazement at his

41

friend Harold Young.

"You turned down a hundred dollars a day? Was you drunk or crazy?"

Jon continued to look with wonder at his old friend. This was something that he'd never heard of before. Here was a man crowding seventy years of age and still in pretty fair shape. He was of medium height and build. He was inclined to be a bit 'paunchy' and he possessed an expressive face with gimlet eyes gazing out at you from a 'ruddy' complexion.

Jon's curiosity had now surpassed his need for another drink. His friend had caught up with him as he was plodding over to another 'watering-place' for a change of pace and scenery.

"Well alright, tell me more," commanded Jon.

"Wa-a-al, it was this way," continued Harold.

"Joe Hodgini was going East with his troup of horses to play the Shrine circus route and he wanted me to go with him and take care of the horses. He offered me twenty five dollars a week so I took it. When I got back off this circut and went back to see Mr. Mugum about the 'White Ticket Wagon' job he had offered me, he said.

'Well Harold I don't think you can get dirty enough on that wagon.'

That was his way of firing me off that job so I had to go back to the reserved seat and encore ticket selling job.

"One summer on the show it rained steady for a week and I remember John Mugum standing in front of the Marquee that featured a large portrait of John Robinson, whiskers and all painted on it.

"Mugum said, 'Well Mr. Robinson if this rain keeps up those whiskers of yours will be down to your knees.'

"The food was always good, the coffee was the best in the world. The cookhouse was the first tent up on the lot in the morning and the first tent down in the evening. The living conditions were not of the best, you slept on a shelf and took your bath out of a bucket.

"Probably the most obstinate cuss on the show was a bear trainer — a Hungarian named John. His bears were always muzzled and he didn't use much cruelty in their

42

training. Just enough to let them emphatically know who was boss. Old John had his left eye clawed out by a bear. He tried to teach a girl called Madam Rasputin to handle his bears. She was supposed to be a daughter of Russia's Mad Monk — Rasputin. It turned out that she was afraid of the bears and John had no patience with her so she was fired. There were four Alaskan Brown Bears in his act.

"Clyde Beatty started as cage boy and worked up to be the greatest wild animal trainer in the world. A movie, 'The Big Cage' was made right out here in Peru's winter quarters. They dressed up the Ring barn with palms to make it look like the jungle. I'd say ninety percent of that movie was shot right out here.

"I knew Tom Mix, Ken Maynard and Hoot Gibson. Ken Maynard was just a big rough cowboy. He married a girl from a wealthy family that lived up around South Bend. Ken was pretty hard to handle. If the ground was the least bit rough he wouldn't come out for fear his horse would stumble. Nick Carter was about the only person who could get along with Ken.

"Never had much to do with the animals, but I do remember the elephants in particular. One time a trainer was taking an elephant down to the river for a bath and the beast turned on him. The elephant picked him up and did a head stand on him using a big rock for a base. That was the end of the trainer. They shot the elephant and the rock was moved to a prominent citizens front yard and is now known as elephant rock.

An elephant chained to a stake don't mean a thing. He can pull up that stake and take off any time he feels like it. When you see an elephant's trunk and tail go up and he starts bellering — look out, he's going to do something and you had better get out of there fast. Never trust an elephant. He's like a mule. A Mule will work for you for twenty years just waiting for the chance to kick your head off.

"We always looked forwards to Sunday. Whatever town we was in we would head for the hotel for a good bath and a good bed. We always got paid on the week-end and we felt as if we could afford it. First chair trumpet got thirty five dollars a week and while I lasted, which wasn't long, I got twenty dollars per week. Trapeze and Perch acts usually drew around a hundred dollars a week. Of course your big names like Tom Mix, the drawing power of the show, would pull down around a thousand a week plus a percentage of the Encore gate.

"Sure wished I'd stayed in that band. I'd probably never have been another Merle Evans but it would have been a damn sight better than selling tickets for the Encore. Now there was a musical genius.

"Merle had played a cornet since he was a youngster and was very good at it. He loved pop-corn and was always munching on the stuff. He was one of the few men who could eat pop-corn and blow high-C on a cornet. This is a tricky feat and could back-fire — stoppage of the horn. Merle spent most of his career playing for the Ringling show. He played his horn with his right hand and conducted the band with his left. He believed the cornet had a more beautiful sound and he was right. A cornet being short has a broad, open and loud tone. The trumpet, it's first cousin, produces a piercing shrill sound.

"The circus band is more or less conditioned for a multitude of surprises and shocks. Any number of mishaps can befall a circus performance and the band must be ready to fill in the gap with appropriate music. This sometimes taxes their ingenuity, especially when a ten horse team, drawing the band wagon with about thirty musicians aboard, decides to run away. The result is chaos as the bouncing wagon is shedding drummers, trombone and clarinet players at every lurch.

"The circus acts do not follow the music, the music is played to accompany the act. The favorite elephant tune was 'Gentry's Triumphal March'. 'High Riding' always accompanied the clown's entrance and they used the 'Anvil Chorus' for the walk-a-round. The disaster song was 'The Stars And Stripes Forever', on hearing this all circus personnel would start clearing the people and animals out of the tent.

"I remember the time when Ben Wallace, Mr. Mugum, Mr. Bowers and John Ringling flipped a coin to see who

44

would own all the circus titles existing between them. John Ringling, representing the Ringling Brothers, agreed to give or take four million dollars for the American Circus corporation or sell his holdings to them. They flipped a quarter down here in the lobby of the Wabash Valley Bank and John Ringling won the toss and bought all the holdings, equipment and titles of 'The American Circus Corp.' It was along about this time that Ben Wallace made the remark; 'I'd give ten thousand dollars to see the German Kaiser standing out there in the street.

"Circus honesty was usually pretty good, oh if anything was stole around here in Peru they always blamed it on the circus folks but this was not anywhere's near true. They had their so called 'Grifters' or 'Boys from Brooklyn' as they were called but they held them pretty much under control.

"If I had it to do over again I don't know whether I'd go back to the circus or not. But I know one thing it's too damn hot to stand out here any longer — I'm gonna cut and run for home. So Long Jon — Take it easy with old John Barleycorn.

LAMOINE MARKS

TRUMAN BUNNELL

Chapter 6

ELEPHANTS & HORSES *Lamoine Marks*
&
Truman Bunnell

Truman Bunnell and his friend Lamoine Marks were standing on the corner watching the parade troupe by. The heat was pretty oppressive but it didn't seem to bother them too much.

Truman turned to his friend and said:

"Too bad there's no elephants in this parade. I kinda miss the sound of their shuffling walk."

"So do I," returned 'Moine'. "They coulda had some of the big beats in the parade just as well as not. Kelly has a few out here in the old winter quarters.

"Speaking of elephants," resumed Truman. "Do you remember the stampede here in Peru? Back in about 1917 I think it was. The elephants were used to parading through down-town Peru. So one day while they were grazing down in the river-bottoms they decided to go on a rampage and hold their own parade.

"They walked up town from the river-bottoms and meandered down main-street, in and out of stores and scaring the hell out of the general populace. The circus folks finally herded them back to the river-bottoms but I guess they had to shoot a few.

"Then there was old 'Dolly'. I remember the time they were using her in some hotel promotional scheme. To get her inside the hotel her trainer would order her to kneel and crawl through the open doors of the establishment. This worked fine on the way in but on the way out, due to his imbibing from his hip flask, he forgot to tell her to kneel. 'Dolly' just walked through carrying the doors, frames and all, with her and scattering glass all over the side-walk.

"Enough of this parade, let's go over to your joint and have a beer." Said 'Moine'.

"Good Idea." Replied Truman. "But say what didja you do to the index finger on your right hand? Ya got it wrapped up like a mummy."

"Opening those damn beer cans with the ring type pop tops."

"You shouldn't be in such a big hurry for a drink that ya cut your finger opening the can. I don't see how ya can read while trying to look over that big tent ya got on your finger."

"OK. Have your fun Truman, but you know I never come to this town for the parade but it takes me back to about the year 1913 when I joined the circus on the Hagenbeck and Wallace show. In fact they were the only show I ever worked for. One of the earliest recollections that stick in my mind was of a Pole wagon bogged down in the mud east of Peru. They hitched fifty horses to it and had an elephant pushing from behind and that wagon moved just like a bull-dozer shoving mud. It was in so deep. They finally gave it up and let it set until the weather cleared and the mud dried up.

"The food on the circus was always excellent but the service depended on the tips your group left with the head-waiter and his crew. If the tips were adequate you ate off the better plates and had nice silverware. The table had a table cloth and your water glasses were filled, sometimes even a bouquet of flowers would be on the table. The coffee cups were of china. But if the tips were poor – so was the service, granite plates, no table cloth and no water.

"So the group would try to find out who was the pimple on the ass of progress. They would search out the culprit in their midst that wasn't fulfilling his obligations and set him straight. After this was accomplished the good service would return. The tips were usually a dollar each for every person in the group per week, this for the head-waiter. And then an additional forty or fifty cents per week for the waiters. This was not high and the extra service was certainly worth the buck and a half a week.

"To get into the cook tent the working class of people had tickets that they presented for their meals. They ate in one side of the tent. The performers and ushers had their meals on the other side of the tent and were admitted by sight. This one man had a fabulous memory and once you were introduced to him he never forgot you. He would admit you to the cook tent from that moment on.

"My only job with the circus was working with the concession group for Nick Carter. I sold pop-corn, candy, souvenirs etc. I was a Candy Butcher in other words.

"Elephants always fascinated me and I loved to watch the training of them. They are very smart and under ordinary conditions they are kind and gentle. The first stages of their training it is necessary to use slings, pulleys and many men to handle them. But once they learn it is very seldom necessary to 'Man-Handle' them again.

"Elephants have a fantastic memory and I believe that if an elephant hadn't been worked for years that a sudden command would put him into a head-stand or whatever else you asked him to do that he had been trained to do. Some of the simpler tricks they will learn in a week while others may take three or four months and working them every day of the month.

"Horses are a different story. They are not so intelligent and it takes considerably more time, patience and tough handling to train them. The whip is the cue for the horse. Not to beat him but to tell him what do do. For instance, you tickle him on the foreleg to get him to strike out and all this time his head is held high in restraint that is extremely uncomfortable for him. When he does what you want him to do on your cue, you release his neck-rein, sponge him off and perhaps give him a carrot as a reward. He soon learns.

"The early American Indians had a unique way of training their horses. Cruel but effective. After catching their horse they would take a piece of wet rawhide and tie it around his upper lip like a 'Twitch', then take him out to some lonely spot in the area and tie him to a rock or tree. They would leave him there for three days without water and food. The horse picks up everything he eats with his upper lip. The 'Twitch' discouraged this. After three days he was so glad to see someone that would take him out of his predicament that he would do anything at all. The Indian could ride him immediately and the horse also knew that from where-ever that 'Twitch' pulled, he'd better mind that and go that way. It was a very effective method of training horses to ride.

"When they taught a horse to stand — ground tied in other words, they would put him in a corral with this 'Twitch' tied to a large cowhide. When he would walk or jump forward he would land on this cowhide thus pulling his head down and hurting his lip. If he jumped backward the cowhide followed him and hurt some more.

"The horse trembles, he sweats and this is a terrible ordeal for him and he fights it for days but he finally learns that it is no use and he will give up. From that day forward he will stand with just the reins from his bridle dangling on the ground.

"Cats, like horses, are not too bright. For training purposes jungle cats are preferred as they have a sort of a natural fear of men which those raised in captivity do not have. While training cats they use a choke collar with a rope and a pulley that is rigged to the top of the arena. The rope is handled by men outside the arena.

"The cat is given his cue and the men pull him up and set him on his pedestal, this is uncomfortable as it chokes him. Over a period of time he will learn that jumping up on the pedestal is a lot less painful and he will obey the cue. Once a lion or a tiger learns his pedestal, that is his pedestal and he will fight to keep it.

"Lions and Tigers have a mutual respect for each other I believe. Pound for pound the Tiger is the King of beasts. A Lion strikes out with his forefeet and dislikes being on his back in a fight. The Tiger loves being on his back and fights with all four feet, he uses his hind feet to rip and tear his adversary's belly.

"The Polar Bear is the toughest animal of all. He is a dangerous cuss and much more intelligent than the cat family. You can look in a cat's eyes and tell what he will do by the dilation of the pupil, a polar bear, no. A certain amount of cruelty is used in the training of all animals. You got to gain their respect and let them know who is boss. Trained animals of any species are hard to buy.

"I remember one giant of a man, a clown, that used only kindness but he was training dogs. He trained Chihuahuas to stand on his hands. One dog standing on his front feet and the other standing on his hind feet—one dog in each hand and he would walk around the hippodrome track that way.

MRS. D. CARTER

Chapter 7

PERFORMER   *Mrs. D. Carter*

Mrs. Carter didn't actively participate in the Circus City parade this year. But over the years, like many others, she financially contributed to the success of the annual Circus City Festival.

In their 'Hey-Day' Mr. & Mrs. Nick Carter lived in a large beautiful home near the center of town. Nick had the gift of turning practically everything he touched into gold. Mrs. Carter, since her husband's passing, sold the palatial pad and moved into a new modern smaller home next door.

She is still a very trim and attractive woman. Time has been kind to her. She has a quick wit, a sharp tongue and, like most women, is a great talker. From a modest birth here in Peru she pursued a successful career in the circus and is now retired and enjoying the hobby of collecting antiques and circus memorabilia.

She was born and raised here in Peru Indiana and evidently the fickle finger of fate singled her out for the circus. One day her mother came home and told her that they were looking for ballet girls to travel with the circus. The pay was fifteen dollars a week plus your board and room. Her mother thought that she could handle the job so she decided to give it a whirl. She joined the Hagenbeck and Wallace show when she was eighteen years old in 1925.

Dortha and her mother cut down an old evening gown to make her first costume. Her mother, an expert seamstress, helped her make her clothes and taught her to be a good seamstress in her own right. A clown taught her the ladder act and to ride a horse. She started out at fifteen dollars a week but with initiative and hard work she climbed up the scale to a 'Prima-Donna' making thirty five dollars a week. She accomplished all of this within the first year she was on the show, and as she says:

"My mother helped me make my wardrobe and you know we made a new one every year. I always sold the previous years' wardrobe to other girls and started out the new circus year with a brand new set of costumes. The only costumes that the circus furnished you was for the tournament, walk-a-round and the Grand Entrance. The clothes you wore in the various acts you had to furnish yourself. I bought the material and did all the sewing.

"The sequins, ornaments, jewels and all decorations were sewed on individually by hand. We even made all our own accessories including pumps by hand. When I was on the road I did have a little sewing machine, a Singer, but you had to turn it by hand power not foot pump power. After I married Nick I had a state-room on the train and could use my spare time revising and making new wardrobes. You also marked all your clothes with your name, this included everything — hat boxes, shoe bags etc.

The timing was so close that one had to be a quick change artist in order to be ready for the cue of the next act. On many occasions we would wear one set of costume underneath the other so all we had to do was strip down to the next attire and pin on a few ornaments. We were then ready for the next act.

"I always enjoyed that circus food, it was marvelous. When the flag went up on the cook tent you eat, when it was down you didn't, you went over on the midway to one of the 'Grease' joints and bought a hamburg.

"I carried my money in a 'Grouch' bag, this is a small crocheted pouch specifically designed to hold money. You always kept your money on your person and never left it laying around in your trunk. It would be stolen sometimes by the town-people who were always wandering around the lot while the show as in progress. I used to carry my 'Grouch' bag in my Bra except when working with the elephants and then I carried it in a little pocket sewn into my tights. The most beautiful 'Grouch' bag I ever had was crocheted by a clown.

"You never heard of a 'Donneker'? Why that is a little brown tent with two toilet seats inside. A tent for the women and one for the men. They put em up, tore em down and covered the hole every day.

"Naturally there were all kinds of tents with the traveling circus. You had the main tent, sideshow, menagerie, cook, baggage, dressing, blacksmith, horses — both performing and stock, and, of course the managers. This amounted to a regular city that was put up and tore down every day, except a lay-over, usually a sunday.

"I believe that the reason the 'tented' circus failed is because now-days it is hard to get the whole family together at one time. Dad is playing golf, Mom's at the bridge club and the kids are bowling or watching T.V. Then too, there's the lack of help, you just can't find enough 'roughnecks' to put up a show. About the only shows that survive in these times are the very small ones, truck shows they call em. That's the way the circuses started out in the very early days, and now that we're back to 'truck-shows' again we've traversed the full cycle. Small to the very big and now back to the small.

"On the road we slept in Pullman cars and were segregated according to our position with the show. Freaks were in one car or a part of one, performers in another and ballet girls in another car. We were always well chaperoned and never allowed to go out with other people. The first time you broke the rules you were fined, the second time you were fired. We slept in bunks — two high, on a shelf we called it and we took our baths in a bucket.

"I married Nick Carter in 1930 and we then moved into a state-room and had much better living conditions. Nick's job with the circus was head porter. He had charge of all the porters and was responsible for all the bunks, blankets and pillows. His salary was small, only about fifteen dollars-a-week but the tips were great. Everyone got a bunk for a small fee. Nick also owned and operated the gambling machines in each car, one armed bandits that is. Oh Yes! He made a great deal of money this way.

"Nick always believed in keeping his wife working. I rode horses for seventeen years both side-saddle and astride. Ya gotta remember one thing when you're working with animals, you follow their cue. You move with the horse and follow his lead and when an elephant moves you'd better be ready.

"The command 'Alright' always precedes a change of pace or a new command to an elephant. You say — 'Alright, sit up', 'Alright, sit down!'; 'Alright go on!' and the elephant will follow through those maneuvers and walk away.

"Before going into the main tent they always ordered the elephants to stand up. This had a tendency to drain them out so they wouldn't dirty the ring. A person could get drowned if they were not drained out. One time I was working with a 'Moon-eyed' elephant that naturally couldn't see very good and she stepped on my arm during a walk-over of me. Lucky for me the lot was soft and my arm just sank into the ground. It barely bruised me.

"I remember a very impressive act that Clyde Beatty used to put on. He would be dressed as a slave girl riding across the saddle of a Sheik who was mounted on a white stallion. Then he was thrown into the den of animals and he would put them through their paces. This always went over big with the crowd. Beatty and I had a lot in common. We had no family to train us and no sponsors in the circus. We sort of came in on a rain check so to speak.

"Tom Mix was a handsome devil. He was part Indian and he took very good care of the people that worked for him. Ken Maynard was a fine fellow, he married a girl friend of mine. Gene Autry, fine man but they tell me some of his nights were sort of fantastic, he was a wild liver. Most theatrical people are Gypsys at heart, they like to be on the go and see action all the time.

Nick and I retired in the forties. I felt I was too old for 'tights' and too young for the peanuts and restaurant circuit. We just found another way to make a living. We got into the beer distributing business and Nick still kept his hand in the concessions. In fact we still have the concessions at the State Fair.

"The concession business is something else again. It's fast and furious and there is plenty of money in it if you watch yourself. We've handled them all: 'Grease-joints, that's hot-dogs and hamburgs. 'Flukes, that's juice, pop and pink lemonade. 'Garbage', that's dolls, flags etc. Still have the concessions at the Indiana State Fair and have had for twenty seven years. Also run Carter's cafeteria and Dorothy's cafeteria there. These are beautifully equipped establishments including steam tables etc.

"But you know it's so hard to get good help now-a-days. You have to hire people that nobody else wants. Anybody worthwhile has usually got a job except the college kids and a lot of them don't want to work. But those that do want to work are excellent and there is never enough of them to go around. In the concession business you gotta be big.

"I never feared the circus 'roustabouts'. We were their queens. Sometimes the sleeping cars were two miles down the tracks in back of some cabbage patch and we had to walk this distance to get to bed but I never was afraid. Those 'roustabouts' were along the way and they looked after us. You feared the town bums more than the circus people.

"In the circus life you tipped everybody that ever did anything for you. You tipped the property men, fellows who looked after your rigging and your groom, the man who saddled your horse. You always tipped these people as they were on a small salary and augmented their income in this manner. If you didn't tip them your saddle might turn on you or a knot slip in the rigging.

"When John Ringling bought the American Circus Corp. at the flip of a coin he ordered everything burned and he shelved the titles as he wanted to be the only show on the road and he didn't welcome competition.

"Old Ben Wallace was quite a guy and he did a lot for Peru. He did have one bad habit though, he loved to chew tobacco and let the juice run down his whiskers."

JOHN SMITH   *PAUL KELLY*

Chapter 8

THE ZOO   *Kelly.*

If you want to see 'The Kellys', other than at the State Fair or a 'Shrine Circus', you will have to travel about six miles southwest of Peru out to the former Terrell Jacobs Winter Quarters. Mr. & Mrs. Kelly, Paul and Dorothy, came to Peru in 1954.

They originally had the idea of a Circus Museum, in 1956 and 1957, and they owned ninteen elephants, thirty some lions and tigers, twenty head of horses, sixteen head of ponies, numerious camels, buffalo, sheep, monkeys, zebras and a hippo. There are many wild animals buried on the property in their animal cemetery including eleven elephants. All that is now left alive on the premises are eight elephants, two seals, two tigers, one lion, a few ponies and a horse.

Three full time people now handle the establishment and care for the animals. The elephants will eat one hundred and twenty five pounds of hay a day each and are grained once a day. They will each drink between sixty and a hundred gallons of water a day. The lions and tigers will eat ten to fifteen pounds of meat a day for six days and on the seventh they are fed milk and eggs to improve their coat.

The Kellys have one baby elephant, two years old, that they run through his paces every day. This young you can man-handle them, without too much difficulty, to get them to obey your commands. This little one is trained with an ordinary man's walking cane. He is treated, like a child, with lots of patience and using a soft spoken voice.

According to Kelly:

"The younger an elephant is when you start the training the better. As they grow older you have to use rigging to make them sit, lay down and move on command. The elephant goad and the spoken word is about all that is used. You have to watch them though as they'll always try to 'short-cut' the trick. If they are supposed to turn around three times they'll turn around twice and hope to get away

59

with it. Don't let them.

"All elephants are run through their paces at least once a week unless they are on 'show', at this time it is usually twice a day. Once-in-a-while you will find an elephant called a runner. A rogue or a sapper balls up his trunk and raps you one. Your only protection is the 'Bull Hook' and watchfulness.

"You can never approach a herd of elephants undetected, day or night and, no matter how small or large the herd. You will always find one or more standing guard while the rest of the herd rests and sleeps. They sleep either lying down or standing up according to their habits. They are very intelligent and there are very few working males in the country. The reason for this is that during their "Teens" the males go through a 'Musk' period and will kill their trainers. At this period they are pretty unmanageable. Most of the trained elephants in this country today are females even if they are called 'Bulls'.

"I once owned a rogue elephant named Kate... She was hard to manage and would try you. Once she learned who was boss though why that was it. We had a hard time teaching her that fact but after that she never 'tried' us again. We had to give her the treatment which was rather brutal. But you know the smarter the animal the harder they are to convince.

"Kate tried to kill me. She reached out with her trunk, grabbed me and pulled me to her. She had to release me in order to do a head-stand on me so when she let go of me I rolled towards another elephant. There were four men in the barn with me. One of them distracted her attention with a broom while the rest of us chained her four feet to rings embedded in the cement floor.

She couldn't break out. We used two by fours and gas pipes and really worked her over. Christianized her so to speak. We beat her until she cried and begged. If you beat them too much you will really make a 'rogue' out of them so we stopped just short of that. And you know she was the best elephant after that beating, she would follow me around like a dog. She recognized her boss and never had to be reminded again.

60

"My father always wanted to own an elephant and never did. I woke up one morning owning fifteen of them. Trained elephants today in this country are in distress for lack of handlers and trainers. A good reliable trained elephant is worth about five thousand dollars. The others that you can't trust you can buy for a thousand dollars or less.

"India elephants are much easier to handle and train. This is probably true because in India they have been training elephants for hundreds of years while in Africa the elephant hasn't been domesticated until quite recently. African elephants are much harder to handle and are weaker physically. You'll find most of your African elephants in Zoos.

"We try never to expose an elephant to under thirty five degress of temperature for any length of time. We haul them around the country by truck unless it is very cold and then we use baggage cars. Coal and oil is used to heat our elephant barn and it costs us about ten dollars a day. We don't heat the cat barn as they will adjust themselves to the temperature.

"Elephants are a lot like humans. They live about seventy years and they mature in their twenties. You know I once heard of an intelligence scale for animals that went something like this. The Dolphin was No. one; Chimpanzee, No. two; About that of a five year old child. Pig, No. three; Elephant, No. four; Dog, No. five; Horse, No. six and Cats No. seven.

"In training the big cats you have to break them by using a collar, chain and a rope that is run through a pulley at the top of the arena. You never reward the cats as you do a horse and the trainer would rather start out with jungle bred cats as they have a fear of man where the 'pets' don't. Mixed groups, lions and tigers, you put together when they are young and once they are broke out or Christianized they'll seldom forget.

"We bought our first seal from a clown named 'Coco', he wanted to return to England and couldn't take the animal with him. This seal was very well trained and she had a sense of humor. We let her have the run of the house and whenever she felt she wasn't getting enough attention she would make for the kitchen, grab a loaf of bread and shake it out of the wrapper all over the floor.

"Seals have a life span comparable to a dog, about fifteen years. You need a large tank of water for their care and each seal will eat about ten pounds of fish a day. We feed our seals perch, whiting and mackerel that is shipped in from Chicago. We also have to supplement the fish diet with vitamins and antibiotics.

"Seals are harder to raise and keep healthy than children. Chlorine in their tank water is bad for them. They do not have to be in the water all the time though it is advisable to keep them moist. They have teeth like a Barracuda and are pretty good fighters. We have trained about eight seals and we now have two left.

"Like children in school, some seals are slow learners and others are more rapid, it takes time and patience. They will bite you but usually a rap on the snoot will cure this. They'll then bawl but they will never bite anybody again. They readily respond to kindness and once started on the road to learning they are very eager. Twice a day we take ours out of the compound to put them through their paces and to feed them.

"The value of a seal out of the ocean and untrained is about one hundred and seventy five dollars. After he is trained, schooled and can do everything in the book he's worth two hundred dollars a day in a show.

"They are very gregarious animals and enjoy company. I remember a time one of our seals got over on a pile of hay that an elephant was eating. The seal rolled over on her back and 'Clapped' her flippers. The elephant went right on eating and payed no attention to the seal, we finally had to call her away.

"Another time I was cutting fish at the table. The seal, loose in the quarters, came over and laid her head in my lap. She watched me chop a few more fish and then she put her head up on the board. I told her 'to move it or I'll cut your whiskers off.' She just rolled those soulful eyes up at me and begged. She got her fish.

"One of our best men still with us is John Smith. He used to ride race horses in his youth. His father was a performer with the P. T. Barnum show.

"Smith changed to training horses for the show ring at a fairly early age and he traveled with all the big shows. He is a firm believer in kindness and repetition in breaking horses. He likes to start with horses that are three to six years old. He trained the 'Liberty' horses with no brutality.

"Peru is a good area to grow hay and that is a basic ingredient for maintaining a circus, this is true today as it was years ago. Many years ago Ben Wallace run a livery stable in this town and a traveling circus couldn't pay their feed bill. So Ben took over the circus and found himself in show business. That was the origin of the Hagenbeck and Wallace shows and the beginning of Peru as a winter quarters.

"The old time circus with all its grandeur and glory is gone forever. About all you now have left are the various Shrine shows throughout the country. Detroit is the 'Grand-daddy' of all Shrine shows, it is good for a seventeen day stand, then on to Minneapolis and Atlanta. Trouble of it is these are usually intermediate dates and not successive. They all try to get into Easter week."

MACLAM

Chapter 9

TONS OF FUN   *Maclam*

Jim was hurring briskly down the street, with his wife in
tow, looking for a vantage point from which to view the
parade. He turned to his wife and said.

"You know hon, The old burg hasn't changed much in
the last thirty years. About the only thing they've added
are those curb-side flower boxes. They make good recept-
acles for cigar butts and gum wrappers.

"How come the gloom is so thick in your eyes that you
could cut it into strips and sell if for viewing eclipses? I
know it is hot but after the parade is over we'll hunt up an
oasis and cool off with a tall drink."

"Here's a good spot," Jim said as he steered his wife
through an opening in the crowd. "It's shady here too."
Jim was all wound up over being at the Circus Festival and
he just had to talk.

"Although Jim Maclam is my name I was known
throughout my time with the circus as 'IRISH'. There was
hardly anyone in the working class of people that was
known by their right names. This was usually true because
of prior circumstances such as running away from home or
dodging the law.

"I joined the circus in 1935 at the age of fourteen. I
ran away from home looking for adventure and I sure
found it working with the elephants. We always called it
the 'Bull' Dept. I guess this was because in bad weather
when all other equipment got stuck the elephants came
through and spotted the wagons and pulled up the canvas.
Many times the elephants moved the show. My job was
cleaning up behind them, swabbing them off, feeding and
watering and putting their harnesses on.

"My pay was three dollars a week and keep. I started
with the Hagenbeck and Wallace show. After being with the
show for nearly a season, about forty weeks, I had a
chance to work the 'Bulls' on the lots and the management
increased my pay to fifteen dollars per week. I finally
worked into 'Ring' helper at twenty five dollars a week and

I really thought I was in the big time. When the end of the season came around I was well enough advanced that they chose me to go into winter quarters with them.

"I took care of the 'Bulls' exercised them and helped train them for new acts. During the winter period we had the opportunity of going out on Shrine Circus dates where we could make up to forty five dollars a week. It was not unusual that extra duties would arise that would allow us to make up to one hundred and fifty dollars a week, and in the late 1930's that was real money. Pay-day was always on Sunday.

"Here elephants are my favorite circus animal and there's not a damn one in the parade. I remember that during storms we always took the elephants outside the tent so they could see what was going on. They love the rain. Lightning and thunder scares them less than the flapping of canvas.

"One time in West Virginia, before we could get the 'Bulls' out, the menagerie tent blew down. Well those damn 'Bulls' stampeded all over town, that is all but two or three of the more sedate and gentle ones. We got on these and rounded up the rest of them. The farmers in the surrounding country reported their location and we went out and got them. Seven miles was about the farthest we had to go to get one 'Bull'. I've heard that elephants love bread and that one was once captured by feeding him twenty four loaves of the stuff, but I donna no."

"Never had many fights while I was on the show. Once in a great while you might hear the yell 'Hey Rube' and that usually meant that some of the city or carnival toughs had started a fight on the circus lot. These people would try to 'Con' our people of both sexes by selling the men 'boot-leg' whiskey and insulting the women. When this happened we-all would just pass by the stake and chain wagon for weapons and dive into the melee.

"Never ate so good in my life, before or since, that circus food was considerably above par — it was absolutely excellent. A lot of guys just worked for food only. While on the road you had a meal ticket and when the flag was up on the cook tent you could eat. You slept in bunks two or three tiers high and the porters took care of the bunks. Oh! It was a good life.

"We had one horse around the 'Bulls', 'Cheerful Gardners.' He would lead the elephants to and from the trains and there was usually a couple of circus dogs that went along for company. Strange dogs were never tolerated around the herd. We had twenty three 'Bulls' that had to be loaded and unloaded daily. They traveled in eight horse cars. I handled the bulls that spotted the wagons in the menagerie tent and also that spotted the wagons in the chutes, to be pulled up on the flat cars of the train at night. They used what they called a 'Galloping Four Horse Hitch' to pull the wagons up the incline.

"We had a 'Dead Herd', these were extra elephants that were being trained for a particular act. But this herd also performed at the final end of the ring act. All the elephants would assemble on the hippodrome track. One elephant would mount his front feet on the rear of the elephant in front. This would continue until all were standing in a line. Then, at an order from their trainer, this formation would be broken and then they would waltz, lay down, sit up and finally grab each other's tails and march out of the tent. All of this was done to music supplied by the circus band.

"When they were not working they were chained in the menagerie tent. We chained their front foot first, stretched them out and then chained their back foot. They were also taught to unchain their front foot, at command, and then turn around and unchain their back foot.

"An ornery young female named 'Mable' once tried to do a head-stand on me. Needless to say I've shied away from that name every since. Well when this happened some woman screamed and that attracted the elephant's attention. I was once told that as soon as you hurt an elephant they are useless.

"I stuck my finger in her eye and rolled out from under her. Other circus hands came to my aid and after chaining her down we sure worked her over with pick handles. We hit her on her toes as that is one place you can usually hurt an elephant.

"Elephants never forget the tricks they learn because of

the constant rehearsing and working the acts. They are trained to follow cues and the bull hook and they will remember their tricks and their handlers for years. After they are completely broken in with the bull-hook, a hook on the end is not necessary. Just any long stick will do.

"Cheerful Gardner could go away from the herd, stand out in a field and call to them, and they would pull their stakes to go to him. They would form a ring and crowd around him. No one else could do this. Some people thought that Cheerful Gardner looked like an elephant but it is pretty evident that he thought like one.

"In addition to feeding, watering and bathing the 'Bulls' I used to have to look after their feet. Periodically I'd take a large rasp and file their toe-nails. I'd put their foot on a pedestal that was about two and a half feet high and then force them to put their weight on the pedestal. This slightly threw them off balance so they couldn't do much without warning us by their weight shifting.

There is also a hole in their head about half way between the eye and ear. This must be kept open and clean and cannot be allowed to close up. I'd have to clean this out about three or four times a year.

"When they heave their body from side to side and have a wild look in their eye it's a danger signal to be heeded. If they are going to run their trunks and tails will be in the air; if about to do a head-stand on you, after throwing you to the ground, their trunk is always rolled up.

"Elephants are mischievous and playful and for that and other reasons their tusks are usually kept sawed off so they won't hurt each other.

"Elephants are always in the same sequence or position in the parade or while walking to or from the trains. The trailing 'Bull' always has a hold of the leading elephant's tail. This is strictly for mind occupation. The handler on the lead 'Bull' is constantly talking to him to keep his mind occupied. The elephant's that is! They also have a strong body odor that freightens horses that are not used to them. Back in the old parade days men on horse-back would precede the elephant herd warning the public to

'Hold Your Horses, the elephants are coming!'

"They eat constantly. There is hay in the cars that they ride in from town to town and there is hay in front of them on the circus lot. Sometimes when we fed them grain they would put their foot on their own pile of oats, then try to eat their neighbors and save their own for later consumption. They love apples, that's one way to find out if an elephant is ill. If he refuses an apple you know he's sick.

"Once heard of an elephant with a king-sized tooth ache. He was sitting on his 'Hiney', swinging his head and really moaning low. Well they chained him down, tied his trunk firmly over his back, bathed the gum of the tooth with cocaine and drilled a hole through it. They then pushed an iron rod through the hole and secured the rod to a rope that was hooked up to a team of horses. At the command of 'Gid-Ap', the horses surged ahead, the elephant reared back and the tooth popped out. You never saw a happier elephant.

"We worked in the movie, 'Here Today And Gone Tomorrow.' The movie people traveled with us through most of the 1936 season. We created scenes typical of every day circus life . . . We thought this was wonderful because of the extra pay that was involved when we got into the action. I also worked in the W. C. Fields' show 'You Can't Cheat An Honest Man.'

"In 1938 I finally decided that this was no life to grow old in so I quit the circus for good — But I still like to come down here and reminisce.

EVA KELLY LEWIS   PAT KELLY
PAT KELLY   PAINTING BY ART JOHN

Chapter 10

THE CLOWN   *Eva Kelly Lewis*

"Yes I was in the circus city parade last year. Do you recall the clown ambling along the parade route, wandering back and forth from curb to curb and leading a little dog on a leash? Well that was me and as long as I'm able I'll be there year after year. Once circus – always circus I say.

"I joined the Gollmar Show back in 1922 and was on that for awhile, then transferred over to the John Robinson show when they came to Peru.

"My sister and I did a double trapeze act, rode horses in the Spec, worked on the swinging ladders and in the Ballet. We didn't make much money and we even had to furnish our own costumes but we sure enjoyed the life.

"The food was always good. The sleeping arrangements left a little to be desired, but we didn't mind that. I had a horse run away with me here in Peru and another time one ran away with me during a parade in Kansas City. A street car scared him and he took off. I couldn't hold him back, just hung on for dear life. Clyde Beatty was the Parade Marshal at that time and he caught up with me and stopped my horse.

"I met Emmett Kelly here in Peru in 1923. We were both on the John Robinson show practicing for a Spec. when we were introduced to each other He clowned and did a single trapeze act. We were married in July.

"You know that clown character and face make up more or less belongs to each clown individual and there is a sort of an unwritten law among clowns that respects this. But since Emmett Kelly became famous there have been a lot of imitators.

"Practically all my people were circus, I had two sisters that were acrobats – top fliers with the Ringling Bros. show. Oh, we had a few mishaps now and then but nothing serious. That is, too very serious. I fell and broke my arm in Traverse City, Michigan. This was right after we got married.

"Pat here, he's following right in his father's footsteps.

He started clowning about nine years ago when he was twenty five or there-abouts. He plays mostly with the Shrine Circuses, parades and a few big Department Stores. He likes the business and he follows his Dad's format pretty close.

"Sad Face Clown. That seems to make the kids the happiest. Clowns are strictly for children. The more ridiculous the act, the better. Kids think it is really funny. One time Pat really broke up, started laughing himself A sad faced clown can't afford that. This happened at Funland at Fort Wayne. Some colored people started to laugh and Pat says he just couldn't help himself and he started laughing too. That was the only time that he ever cracked up and had to laugh at himself.

"You always work towards the children. You pick out a child and project yourself towards him, try to make him laugh. Sometimes it isn't easy, as they may be leery or slightly afraid. Being a clown is hard work. To begin with, you spend up to an hour or more getting ready for the act; dressing and putting on your make-up is time consuming. Then the show lasts for two or three hours and, in the case of the Shrine Circus you sometimes have three shows a day."

Pat spoke up and said: "In Washington, D.C., I played to a group that included an astronaut's daughter. I thought that was a special occasion and we did our very best, got a lot of laughs, too.

"A few years ago I was parade marshal in Sudan, Kansas, my father's home town. He was born and raised there before moving to Kansas City, Mo. Dad finally broke away from the double trapeze act and went into clown character. He tried quite a few before deciding on the present format. Dad's now crowding seventy years of age."

Mrs. Eva Kelly Lewis once again picked up the conversation, as she said, "I remember one time when we were all on the hippodrome track making a walk-a-round Spec. when one of the clowns hollered — 'My God, I've lost my grouch bag and all my money's in it.' He immediately left the Spec. and raced back to the dressing room to look for it. Lucky man, he finally found it and his money was

72

there.

"Another time while I was on the John Robinson show we had an act that included girls dancing inside simulated vases. Incense was burning over the top of the vase while the Band played for the dance. Then the vase opens up and in the process one of them tipped over and the young lady's pants caught fire. She ran out of the tent hollering for help and the crowd thought it was all part of the act. But it wasn't supposed to be and it wasn't really funny although the crowd laughed. You know, that girl had third degree burns.

"One summer in Oil City, Pennsylvania, Terrell Jacobs' lions got out. I was on the trapeze when they hollered — 'Lions are out!' I just held onto the rope, afraid to come down. In the resulting confusion the monkeys also gained their freedom and one girl performer climbed on top of a cage wagon and screamed — 'My God, I'm more afraid of the monkeys than I am the lions.'

"Some of our colored Roustabouts were down by the river doing their washing. One of them was pounding his clothes on a rock when he looked up and said: 'My Lord A-mercy, there's a lion.' The other one turned around and said, 'I can't swim, but I'm sure gonna now' and he dove in the river. His buddies finally fished him out of the stream and Terrell got his lions back in their cages. Another time a lion got loose during a parade in Richmond, Va. The lion jumped on a horse's back and started chewing his neck. The cops shot both the lion and the horse.

"Terrell Jacobs was quite a man and a great animal trainer. He sorta believed that dumbness was not in the animal but in the owner. He kept his voice on an even tone, kind and yet stern. He had patience, patience and still more patience. He believed that you should never lose your temper and that the whip should never be used as an instrument of chastisement or to instill fear in the animal. The whip was used as a cue such as tapping a horse on the forelegs to get him to kneel. Tap him on the nose or jaw to get him to rear or do a walk on his hind legs. Terrell Jacobs once said that 'Kindness and Patience is the Golden Rule of animal training.'

73

"What animal trainers fear the most are the deep wounds caused by clawing and not an attack by teeth or fang. Terrell once found himself at the bottom of a pile of four fighting lions. This occurred in the winter quarters of the old Hagenbeck and Wallace show while he was breaking in a new lion act. His daring, cool headedness and a loaded gun tossed to him by an assistant enabled him to separate the fighting lions and restore peace in the arena. But after this episode he spent a few delirious days in Peru's Duke hospital.

"Mable Stark, a tiger trainer, turned her back on a cat that she trusted. The cat got her and then another one joined in the fray. Her assistants finally beat the cats off with grubbing hoes. But they had torn her leg up pretty bad. And you know — she was a registered nurse; she sewed up her own leg.

"Yes, I believe the old circus days are more or less gone forever even though the Ringling shows are going on the road this year in March. They have two shows called the Red and the Blue. It's pretty hard to get enough roustabouts to work cheap enough to handle a show."

The
Bearss House

In 1834, soon after the town of Peru was "laid out", Daniel Bearss paid $150. for the lot, 60 feet by 132 feet, where the Bearss House now stands. Soon after, a tavern was constructed on the site.

In 1835 the price of a venison steak dinner was 25 cents and the price of a bed was one shilling. A supply of logs, suitable for splitting into rails, was kept in the rear yard, and the traveler who might be short of funds could split rails to pay for his room and board, at the rate of 25 cents per hundred. Fence rails were in demand to fence the yards and vegetable gardens of the early residents of Peru. Livestock, in those days, roamed at will.

In 1836, when the relatives of Frances Slocum came to Peru in an endeavor to have her return with them to Wilkes Barre, Pa. she would not come from her home at "Deaf Man's Village" to the meeting place, the tavern now occupied by the Bearss Hotel, until "Squire James Fulwiler" agreed to attend the meeting. She trusted him to support her desire to remain with the Miamis.

In 1880 Mr. Kumler and Mr. Graves became the proprietors and named the hotel the Bearss. It had previously been known as the Broadway House.

A business directory, published in 1896, lists the Bearss House as a leading hotel, and the Bearss Sample Room as one of the better vendors of "firewater". The Innkeeper was W.V. Turpen.

In 1901 the Shively Brothers purchased and operated the cigar counter.

In recent years, the "Vikings" have invaded the site and the genial Swedish Innkeeper, Hans Kohler, is now the host at this historic hostelry. The Red Coach Room is fast becoming a favorite meeting place for the local folks as well as the tourists.

Now known as the Peru Motor Lodge, it reflects the changes in transportation that has taken place in one hundred thirty years, from the Pirogue of the French explorer to the Jet Age, yet still retaining the famous hospitality and excellent food and drink of a bygone era.

Peru Motor Lodge

FARRELL BROWER

BILL SHANKS   BILL DEVINE

EPILOGUE

There is much humor as well as pathos in the history of Peru's winter quarters. It goes without saying that the owners of a show had hard and fast rules and none of them were flexible. Each and every person connected with a show knew their job and they did it.

There were a few occasions when some of the circus personnel over-stepped their so called job-descriptions and responsibilities, and, the owners didn't find out about it until the deed had been accomplished. For instance:

There is a story that persists that the Elk Statue standing on the top of the Elk's lodge was purloined from the lawn of a prominent citizen living in a western state. An individual known as "Hog Jaw Fats" borrowed it, put it in the elephant car for the ride back to Peru, then set it up again at the Ben Wallace diggings.

Perhaps one of the saddest events occurring here was the great destruction of circus wagons on November 21st in the year 1941. They were ordered burned when management decided to close out that phase of the winter quarters and put the land up for sale. This was a tragic day in the minds of circus wagon lovers. Many circus fans tried in vain to buy some of these wagons but management refused.

The people of this little Indiana town take great pride in their circus heritage and are doing everything they possibly can to preserve and carry on their legacy.

All the characters in this book, except one, are still living here in Peru and, in the past, were an integral part of the various circuses that wintered here. There are also many other people living here that were a part of the circus but time, space and various other reasons did not permit their inclusion in this book. And my thanks goes out to all of you.

And in closing — I wish to extend my appreciation and

thanks to Farrell Brower, Chad Ballard, Wilbur Smith, Bill Shanks, Mrs. Dr. Meeker and Bill Devine for their assistance in arranging the necessary interviews with the people that appear in the book.

Don L. Chaffee

About The Author

Don L. Chaffee was born in Greenville, Michigan. Having graduated from Greenville public schools, he studied engineering at Michigan State University, took up vocational studies at the Watervliet and Watertown Arsenals, and business administration in Grand Rapids.

In college he played the trumpet in the varsity band. During the 1930s he was a barnstorming pilot, performing at county fairs and elsewhere. For years he was employed on quality control and as an inspector in various aeronautical plants, private and governmental.

Mr. Chaffee's son, Roger, an Apollo astronaut, was one of the victims of the tragic fire in the test Apollo spacecraft at Cape Kennedy.

At present, Mr. Chaffee is a real estate broker. **INDIANA'S BIG TOP** is his second published novel. He is the well known author of *MORE THAN BREAD,* also co-author of his son's biography *ON COURSE TO THE STARS* published in January of 1968.